Words, Phrases and Short Sentences

영영 영어회화 500

초판 1쇄 인쇄 2021년 2월 15일
초판 1쇄 발행 2021년 2월 20일

지은이 명광식
펴낸이 金泰奉
펴낸곳 한솜미디어
등록   제5-213호

편집   박창서 김수정
마케팅 김명준
홍보   김태일

주소   05044 서울시 광진구 아차산로 413
        (구의동 243-22)
전화   02) 454-0492(代)
팩스   02) 454-0493
이메일 hansom@hansom.co.kr
홈페이지 www.hansom.co.kr

값 8,000원
ISBN 978-89-5959-537-2 (03740)

* 잘못 만들어진 책은 구입하신 서점에서 바꿔드립니다.
* 이 책은 아모레퍼시픽의 아리따 글꼴을 사용하여 편집되었습니다.

Words, Phrases and Short Sentences

영어회화 영영 500

명광식 지음

한솜미디어

| 머 리 글 |

『영영 영어회화 500』을 출간하면서

이 책은 필자가 미국에 유학하여 60여 년을 생활하며 얻은 언어 체험을 바탕으로 쓴 책입니다. 미국인들이 일상생활에서 자주 사용하는 단어나 문구, 문장을 초보자도 알기 쉽게 체득할 수 있도록 집필한 책입니다. 미국의 일상 TV나 라디오 방송, 출판 매체에서 자주 이용하는 표현 가운데 500개를 선정 그 의미를 쉬운 영어로 설명한 영영英英회화 '가이드 북' 같은 책입니다.

아무쪼록 이 작은 책자가 학생이나 일반인들이 영어를 현지인의 감각으로 이해하고 구사하는 데 도움이 되기를 바랍니다.

2021년 2월

명광식

| Begin forwarded message |

Dear readers,

Recognizing the English is the most widely spoken
language in the world, this book makes an attempt
to help the beginning level of second language speakers
to learn and get familiar with words, phrases and
short sentences often expressed in the media,
namely on television, radio and in the publications.

What's in this book are:

The collection of widely used and spoken words
in the media and in ordinary discourse.

Illustrations of structuring words in a sentence:
to get you, the second language speakers,
familiar with arranging words in an orderly form.

Explaining the difficult words by means of everyday words in layman's terms.

Try to make the second language speakers to understand new words in English without resorting to the first language.

Sincerely yours,

Kwang S. Myung

ENGLISH

1

How do you see it from your perspective (= a point of view)**?**

2

Shopping in person (= personal presence)

3

Doing good/bad/great/well (= doing OK or not OK)

4

Getting better/worse (= improving or not improving)

5

Get the job done (= finish the work)**!**

6

It is within reach (= close enough)**.**

7

Tuning him out (= stop listening or paying attention)**.**

8

Will get worse before they get better (= continue to get worse).

9

Rip off someone/customers (= cheat or steal).

10

He carries bully pulpit (= a position that allows to express beliefs or opinions to many people).

11

We heard of it many times before (= deja vu).

12

Throw a monkey wrench (= sabotage).

13

Just hours away from the deadline (= close to deadline).

14

They have reached a deal on a nearly $100.00 billion package (= have agreed on a nearly $100.00 billion deal).

15

It is alarming (= worrying).

16

Reached the highest in 10 years (= reached a peak in 10 years).

17

Struggling to make ends meet (= earn enough money to live)

18

This is out of bounds (= beyond prescribed limits).

19

This is not rocket science (= something that is difficult to learn or understand).

20

They railroad me into doing it (=force me into doing something without enough information)**.**

21

He received vaccine (=vaccinated) **in television appearance** (=appearing on television)**.**

22

We just hang around with old friends (=just relaxing without doing any particular thing)**.**

23

Just hang on to it (=just continue doing)**.**

24

He can land it (=can get it done as prearranged or can do it)**.**

25

Her speech was an eye-opener (=something that teaches people in a surprising way) **for us. We Learned a lot of things that we didn't know.**

26

Call it a sham (= meant to deceive people or fraud).

27

He is bad to the core (= extremely bad or rotten to the core).

28

Way too high (= very high)

29

Start fresh today (= begin something again).

30

Baked in the system (= already in there)

31

A life well lived (= had a good life).

32

Hang in the balance (= uncertain)

33

Armed with misleading data (= having bad data)

34

It is personal to me (= private).

35

It was a game changer (= a significant shift).

36

Tuck in the shirt (= put back the hanging out part into the pants).

37

This is an uncharted territory (= we have never been/something new/not yet explored).

38

He has spine to say no (= he has gut to say no/ has courage to say).

39

Fray around /at the edges (= becoming weaker/less effective)

40

It is only just a matter of time (= it is certain to happen).

41

Throw it into chaos at 11th hour (= at the last minute).

42

Now more than ever (= more than any time before)

43

Certainly confusing and causing chaos (= messy conditions)

44

He is as American as apple pie (= typical American, real American or average American).

45

A mess of epic proportions (= huge/massive extent)

46

Good riddance (= glad that it's gone)**!**
Winter is finally over (= finally gone)**.**

47

Stand up to bullies (= resistant to bullies)

48

It still has room for it (= it has a space for it)**.**

49

Did you get a heads-up (= hint, alert)**?**

50

Made some headway (= progress) **with the project.**

51

Headwinds (= obstacle) **in business**

52

You got to stand up and say enough is enough (= no more).

53

Let's switch gears (= change subject) **and discuss other things.**

54

It goes without saying (= no further explanation is necessary).

55

Garbage in, garbage out (= bad goes in, bad comes out-it's natural)

56

Root cause (= core source of something)

57

The best way forward (= the best option)

58

A path forward (= a particular type of action to lead to success)

59

Good at dangling (= offering something to persuade someone to do something)

60

Humane way to help (= gentle or kind way)

61

Rotten to the core (= completely bad)

62

He is being accused of having double standards (= favors one person or group over another).

63

Just a pipe dream (= just fanciful hope)

64

A no-go for today (= not doing today)

65

Live coverage (= a broadcast of an event while the event is happening)

66

Spin out of control (= uncontrollable)

67

He bungled badly in planning (= made mistakes in planning)

68

Making a return to a more traditional way (= a return to a normal and ordinary way)

69

Laser focused (= focusing like a laser: concentration)

70

Hype it up (= make people get excited)

71

Keep people afloat (= enough money to live)

72

Get up to speed (= catching up to do)

73

Open your heart (= be generous)

74

It was just a theatrical gesture (= just to get attention, not sincere)

75

She sides with him (= she favors him over someone else)

76

She tried to make amends (= to correct a mistake) **by apologizing to him.**

77

Stories that matter you (= stories that concern you)

78

It's far from over (= not near the end)

79

A defining moment (= the time that reveals what something is really all about)

80

Cut out for something (= suited for something): **He is not cut out to be a teacher.**

81

In time (= early enough): **we got to the class just in time. I want to be at the airport in time to see his departure.**

82

A silver lining in a gloomy situation (= something good happens in a bad situation)

83

Don't leave them twisting in the wind (= to be left in a difficult or problematic situation).

84

Don't make the same mistakes over and over again (= repeating the mistakes).

85

He gave them a leg up (= a boost)**.**

86

There was no daylight between the two points (= a difference)**.**

87

We have to be there before daylight (= daybreak)**.**

88

His ability to do the job is in question (= uncertain)

89

He has it in his DNA (= born with it)**.**

90

Back to you (= return to you)

91

Dial up attacks (= increase attacks)

92

This time, your rhetoric really crossed the line (= went over the limit).

93

Can you knock a week off (= shorten a week)?

94

This meal paled in comparison to yesterday's lunch (= was not nearly as good as yesterday's).

95

In-depth report details chaos (= confusion, turmoil).

96

Let's get this all wrap up (= conclude).

97

A new year is more like closing an old chapter and opening a new one (= fresh start).

98
That should be on the top of mind (= the first priority).

99
The problem has been ignored by us for far too long (= a long time).

100
A situation could blow up in your face (= could have a bad result that you did not expect).

101
It is in limbo (= uncertain stage)

102
Allowing it to lapse (= to end)

103
Who coined that phrase (= create that phrase)?

104
I felt gross (= very disgusting).

105

This project is moving ahead at warp speed (= very high speed).

106

What we hope for in 2021 is world peace (= we want world peace in 2021).

107

He is trying to do something meaningful on the way out (= to leave something to remember him)

108

Just took everyone by surprise (= everyone got surprised).

109

Together we can go further (= do more).

110

My heart goes out to those victims (= feel sorry).

111

Out of sequence (= not in order)

112

A period of disharmony (= discord) **within the two people.**

113

Rollout begins today (= the first offering).

114

Binge drinking on rise (= too much too often).

115

We will beat him at the ballot box (= we will vote him out).

116

Pushed to the brink (= the edge)

117

The crash causing backups (= delays) **on the road.**

118

He tries to remember that sound bite (= a phrase used or broadcast during a news program or a short catchy comment or saying)**.**

119

Hedging their bets (= protect their bets)

120

After he opposed it, he backpedals (= retreats) **and approves it.**

121

He said loudly "heads up" (= look up) **as he threw a stone high into the sky.**

122

You put the nail on the head (= saying what is exactly right)**.**

123

Finding the ways to repurpose the old equipment (= to use it for a different purpose)

124

It is a long shot (= the chances of winning are very rare).

125

All hands-on deck approach is needed to do this job (= the involvement of all members of a group is a must).

126

Read the tea leaves (= see the small signs to predict what is coming up).

127

He is levelheaded (= ability to think clearly and make right decisions).

128

We need a cool head in a crisis (= calm demeanor).

129

It is worth noting (= here is something you should pay attention to or remember) **that he was born in Korea, not a native American.**

130

This is our moonshot (= an exceptionally ambitious project)**.**

131

We have a huge backlog (= an accumulation of uncompleted work to be finished)**.**

132

It is under the microscope (= being studied or watched very closely)**.**

133

Give a reality check (= fact check)**.**

134

Got stuck with (= no progress, difficult to move forward)

135

An unvarnished counsel (= plain, honest advice)

136

Pay tribute to (= express respect)

137

He doesn't know the bounds (= the limit of what is right or wrong)

138

We have to flush out (= force something out of a place or hiding) **the unwanted things.**

139

You need to flesh out (= provide more information) **your story with more details.**

140

He is acting/behaving /moving erratically (= inconsistent, not usual).

141

Some of investigations end up with dead ends (= leads to nothing further).

142

How do you go about trying to address those issues? (= how you handle those problems?)

143

When I look back (= think of the past) **I can see where we went wrong.**

144

They hollowed out (= dig and remove the inside of something) **a tunnel through the mountain.**

145

Your prediction was spot-on (= exactly right).

146

The bill's fate (= it's future) **in the Senate is uncertain** (= unclear or may not pass the Senate).

147

We need to retool (=improve) **the way we use words and phrases to keep up with its new trend.**

148

It sent into frenzy (=excited and uncontrollable state)**.**

149

There are many automobile graveyards (=where junk like old automobiles and broken machines are stored or thrown away)**.**

150

The new ad has helped to stoke (=increase) **sales.**

151

Stoke (=stir up or add fuel to) **violence.**

152

Lawmakers are filibustering (=making a long speech) **to delay the vote.**

153
He is gaslighting you (= making you doubt what you are doing or sowing doubt in you)**.**

154
It is merely a one-time check/deal (= just this one only)**.**

155
People from all walks of life (= refer to all of the people who have different jobs or positions in society)**.**

156
Nothing short of irresponsible behavior (= close to irresponsible action)

157
Encountering roadblocks (= facing obstacles)

158
Now it is time to step up to the plate (= face it) **and do something.**

159

His announcement quickly garnered 100,000 likes (= collected).

160

There is growing pressure on all sides to act (= under increasing pressure to do something).

161

They were showered with book deals and speaking gigs (= got an abundance of something).

162

My patience begins to run out (= been used, finished or no longer endure/tolerate).

163

We got your work cut out for you (= prearranged something for you to do).

164

No fault of his own (= not because of him)

165

He felt great empathy with/for/toward the poor (= the feeling that you understand and care about them).

166

We see a light at the end of the tunnel, but it is far away yet (= it will take some time to get there).

167

For those left out in the cold (= for those abandoned)

168

A nail-biting waiting period (= difficult, worrying period)

169

He has not yet found his groove (= a state in which he is able to do something well).

170

He cracked the case (= broke, solved, found a crime)**.**

171

Kept under wraps (= kept secret)**.**

172

Fight like hell (= really fight using a lot of effort)**.**

173

Stock (= fill) **his staff with his high school classmates.**

174

We will get through (= overcome) **this problem.**

175

They go hand in hand (= closely connected)**.**

176

He lives in the past (= thinking too much about the past believing things are the same as they were in the past)**.**

177

Rollout underway (= a significant release)

178

The real bottom line (= ultimate outcome)

179

Reporters are scrambling (= move or act quickly) **to finish stories before deadline.**

180

The new evidence clinches (= make certain, finalize) **the case.**

181

Even when she answers a difficult question, she minces no words (= speak in a direct way without worrying that she may be offending someone)**.**

182

What he said put the world on pause (= stop and think about something seriously)**.**

183

Don't say it if you think that will draw somebody's ire (= make someone angry)**.**

184

When you see people do nice things, take a moment and give them shoutout (= praise)**.**

185

He is gone. Well, good riddance (= better off without him)**!**

186

The storm is making its way up the East Coast (= heading toward the East Coast)**.**

187

Allowing legal abortion will signal paradigm shift (= an important pattern change) **in Latin America.**

188

How cold will it get in your area (= how cold is it going to be in your area)

189

As quickly as humanly possible way (= by all means).

190

During the last several years we have seen many changes took place in the political landscape (= scene).

191

A torrential rainstorm (= a sudden, violent outpouring) **prompted us to evacuate.**

192

No absolute obligation to enroll (= no need to enroll).

193

You are next in line at the store (= you are next after the person in front of you).

194

I have got your back (= am prepared to help whenever you need).

195

There is zero efficacy (= not effective).

196

Today is December 30. We are going to close out (= end) **this year 2020 soon.**

197

The payments will start hitting your bank account (= will be deposited) **soon.**

198

As soon as he okays it, I will get the wheels turning (=make it start).

199

It has no realistic path to quickly pass the Senate (=no quick way to pass it through the Senate).

200

Does he deserve such a generous treatment, considering the company's subpar performance (=below average)?

201

We are considering whether to re-up (=renew) **our gym membership for next year.**

202

It is a monster storm (=extremely large).

203

They fought tooth and nail (=with a lot of determination).

204

He laid the bait (= trap) **and the media took it, the misinformation spreads.**

205

You have to see it to believe it (= you are not going to believe it unless you see it).

206

Easy come, easy go (= if you win easily you can also lose as easily). **His attitude for money has always been easy come, easy go.**

207

Do not cut corners (= doing badly, cheaply or skipping the requirements) **when time is short to finish the project.**

208

He tossed out her suggestions (= threw it out, did not accept).

209
I will even toss in (= throw in) **some nice extras for free.**

210
Arrange a helicopter to pick us up the moment we land (= as we land)**.**

211
He spoke at length, punctuated (= interrupted) **by frequent applause.**

212
He is literally hanging on by a thread (= very close to death, failure)**.**

213
I was kinda (= kind of) **sorry to see you broke your ankle.**

214
At the last minute we are having a lot of problems that are bigger than previously thought (= we need to do a careful planning)**.**

215

I have been on the go (= very busy) **all this afternoon.**

216

I have fixed that problem in no time (= very quickly)**.**

217

That is an over-the-counter medicine (= you can get it without a prescription)**.**

218

Taking that as a hostage (= hold as a security) **until they get what they want.**

219

The election is still days away (= many days until election day)**.**

220

I will equate (= the same as) **that hack to act of war.**

221

The book was pared down (= reduce) **to 200 pages.**

222

We can't take much more (= too much to handle)**.**

223

You still have a few hours left to finish a few things before 2020 is gone (= you still have time to put closure to that matter)**.**

224

Everyone was kept in the loop (= kept informed)**.**

225

Our suggestion was immediately rebuffed (= refused)**.**

226

They are all ready to battle it out (= fight it out until there is a definite winner)**.**

227

They were turning over every rock, leaving no stone unturned (= a thorough investigation or search).

228

Things are still very fluid (= not fixed, likely to change).

229

We have zeroed in on our study (= concentrate, focus on).

230

Off the top of my head (= without thinking too much, according to my memory), **I would say we have about 100 guests.**

231

The reporter claims that he has the inside dope on him (= information that is not commonly known).

232

Give me the straight dope on the matter (= tell me the true story).

233

She always knows the scoop (= information known only by a particular group).

234

I am really worn out (= really exhausted).

235

Who is going to put the finishing touch (= finalize)?

236

He has set aside (= save it for later use) **some money for his child education.**

237

Everybody was in on it (= participated in).

238

It is getting late, so let's shove off (=leave a place)**.**

239

Shove it (=you will not deal with it)**.**

240

He gave the door a shove (=forceful push) **to open it.**

241

It was a hard lesson (=learned through experience and by making mistakes)**.**

242

It was powerful, uplifting story (=encouraging story)

243

I had a hell of time (=difficult time) **trying to finish that project on time.**

244

That was one hell of a party (=good, impressive).

245

He is one hell of a guy (=very pleasant).

246

Heavy rains ease fires (=give some relief) **but causes flooding.**

247

He is always willing to lend his friends a hand (=help, assist).

248

Since the recession, the company has been teetering on the brink of closing down (=going out of business).

249

He talks about hypotheticals (=imaginary rather than something real).

250

First, here is my take (= my opinion).

251

There is no silver bullet (= a magical shot) **to prevent it.**

252

That is not the decision that I made lightly (= easily).

253

This, to me, seems to indicate that they are getting cold feet (= a feeling of doubt or worry) **in what they have done so far.**

254

Let's kick it into higher gear (= a faster pace).

255

Let's get it all out (= do with as much as effort as possible).

256

We hope this success story will have snowball effect (=become larger, causes many other similar events)**.**

257

Your suggestion is a great one. I am sold (=persuaded)**.**

258

He is trying to curry favor (=gain favor) **with the voters by promising a tax cut.**

259

You put me in a tight spot (=a difficult or embarrassing position)**.**

260

He repeated the point twice just to drive it home (=make people understand the point)**.**

261

We will nail down (=make it certain to happen) **the date for a visit.**

262

Break away from the group (= leave the group).

263

This case happened within living memory (= during a time that people can remember).

264

Turning up the heat (= increasing pressure).

265

What is more American than baseball and apple pie (= all traditional Americans love baseball and apple pie)**?**

266

We saw the writing on the wall (= a sign that something will happen or about to happen).

267

The last question on the test was toughie (= tough one).

268

He broke rank to vote for his friend (= fail to maintain unity or solidarity)**.**

269

Business as usual approach (= the way always we do)**.**

270

If you do that, your head will be on a spike (= will destroy you)**.**

271

He will go inside her head (= find out what she thinks)**.**

272

The most ambitious plan in modern U.S. history is off to a slow start (= starting slowly)**.**

273

Tensions heat up (= tensions increase) **between the two nations.**

274
His illness precipitated a family problem (= factors that caused something to occur).

275
Most insured pay zero dollar (= insurance pays for the insured).

276
Was he able to change any minds (= thoughts, decisions).

277
He was on the home stretch (= the final part of an activity).

278
What is the biggest takeaway (= the main point) **from the lecture?**

279
It sounds the alarm (= warning: you warn people of danger).

280

Hit the blank wall (=further progress is impossible).

281

A one-on-one review (=directly involving only two people).

282

Thank you all for being here (=all your presence).

283

His story has fallen apart (=collapse, becomes disorganized).

284

We were counting down (=paying attention to) **the miles as we approach the finish line.**

285

Let's not beat around the bush (=avoid talking about something difficult).

286
We will cross that bridge when we come to it (= telling someone not to worry about something that has not happened yet)**.**

287
They want to drag it out (= delay) **for a month.**

288
He went on and on··· (= continue)**.**

289
He spilled the beans (= reveal secret unintentionally)**.**

290
It's all up in the air (= nobody knows what will happen next)**.**

291
Taxes are cut to kick-start (= happen more quickly) **the economy.**

292

Felt blindsided by it (= caught unprepared)**.**

293

Something akin (= very similar, related) **to it.**

294

Figure out which is which (= find out which is the one)**.**

295

He is a mind reader (= know what one think)**.**

296

He raised eyebrows over some of the suggestions (= cause you to feel surprised)**.**

297

That looks fishy (= looks strange, causing doubt)**.**

298

Her response to the question was very telling (= reveal her real feeling)**.**

299

At the outset (= beginning).

300

As clear as two plus two equals four (= no doubt).

301

Turn it down a notch (= decrease its intensity, slow down).

302

His moods change from one extreme to another (= he is an extremist).

303

The organization has grown in stature (= level of respect) **during her time as president.**

304

The forest was devoured (= destroyed, consumed) **by fire.**

305

Devouring (= enjoying) **the scene before him.**

306

He is neck and neck (= having equal chance of winning) **with her.**

307

He always left work feeling fatigued (= tired)**.**

308

You can bank on (= rely on, depend on) **my support.**

309

Vote him out of office (= remove)**.**

310

Don't dwell on (= think about it too long) **the past.**

311

My computer went haywire (= not working properly)**.**

312

He had let us down (= failed to support when help is needed)**.**

313

A telling moment (= producing strong emotions)**.**

314

This is wide open race (= anyone can win)**.**

315

The game proved to be a slam dunk (= sure to happen, easy win) **for our side with a 12 to 3 win.**

316

Sitting in awe (= a feeling of wonder)

317

He was awed (= overwhelmed) **by the natural beauty of the mountain.**

318

He is an open-minded (= willing to listen to different ideas and opinions) **guy.**

319

A sold-out show (= all seats are being sold).

320

It is very difficult to debate with closed-minded (= having a mind unreceptive to new ideas) **person.**

321

He told us a real whopper (= a big lie).

322

I think it was a theatrical gesture (= not genuine or sincere just to get attention).

323

It looks like the anger boiling up (= becoming violent, very angry) **inside him.**

324

Someone was able to slip through (= sneak in) **the guard and slip out** (= move out of the place without being noticed) **the back door.**

325

I did not intend to tell them, but it just slipped out (= said by mistakes)**.**

326

Make sure you don't slip up (= make a mistake) **again.**

327

Dodging the questions (= avoiding questions)**.**

328

Simply a matter of right and wrong (= either right or wrong)**.**

329

Build a grassroots movement (= organize and mobilize people to influence political and social issues)**.**

330
The stench of corruption (= a bad smell of being corrupted)

331
No sweat! (= no trouble, can be done easily).

332
We can back it up (= support).

333
Their sadness is manifest on their faces (= clearly visible).

334
Off the track (= away from one's train of thought).

335
He went through hell (= bad time).

336
Stomach- churning stories (= causing disgust)

337

She shook her head in disgust (=dislike) **when I told her what happened.**

338

It is in a state of flux (=constantly changing)**.**

339

It is music to his ears (=something that is gratifying to hear)**.**

340

A perceived threat (=thought of being threatened)

341

We are continuing to progress except for a slight hiccup (=a small problem) **earlier this month.**

342

How's things (=how are things going)**?**

343

We want to resolve this headache without resorting (= without using force) **to force.**

344

He is always willing to do their bidding (= do one is told to do)**.**

345

Throw cold water on (= to prevent from being carried out)**.**

346

What is your personal credo (= philosophy, guiding principle)**?**

347

Size up a situation (= carefully think about the situation so that you can decide what to do)

348

Stone silence (= completely silent, as silent as a stone)

349

Surfing on the internet (= looking for the information or other interesting things)

350

You talk too much. Just give me a talking point (= something to talk about)**.**

351

We have a few days of gloomy weather (= not sunny)**.**

352

His tale of crossing the border was riveting (= exciting)**, but I wonder how much is fiction.**

353

We left him out in the cold (= ignored, excluded)**.**

354

They beat around the bush (= talk about lots of unimportant things) **to avoid confronting real issues.**

355

Say what is on your mind (= concerned about)**.**

356

We have them under our sway (= we control them)**.**

357

He persisted in his argument, but I didn't let him sway (= make me agree) **me.**

358

It is very hard to believe such behavior is still tolerated in this day and age (= in current times: nowadays)**.**

359

We have solved the problem thanks to (= because of) **his input.**

360

He resists to drilling down (= examine in depth) **into the details of his discussion.**

361

I am old-fashioned (= not modern)**.**

362

He is fired up (= exited, enthusiastic)**, but not ready to go.**

363

A lot going into my calculus (= calculation, thinking) **to decide on next step I should take.**

364

It is certain to draw fire (= backfire) **from everyone there if he says those things lightly.**

365

The truth is that it mortified (= make one feel embarrassed and foolish) **me to have to admit that I have never been there.**

366

He is capable of walking and chewing gum (= able to do two things at the same time) **while doing a complicated job.**

367

He reasoned out (= found a solution to) **the problem by thinking out** (= consider all the possibilities and the details of it)**.**

368

Siding with good guys over bad ones (= support one side, the taking of sides; partisanship)**.**

369

He always goes extra miles (= do more) **in an effort to find a solution.**

370

He is set to inherit an organization compromised (= weakened) **by hack.**

371
He could not hack (=deal with) **the new things.**

372
It really hacks me off (=make one angry or annoyed)

373
She is on track (=likely to be successful) **to remain in the current role.**

374
Tensions flare (=burst out, begin something suddenly)

375
What is all about (=real purpose of something)**?**

376
He took a deep breath to fortify (=make feel less fearful) **himself before stepping onto the stage.**

377

Let the process play out (= to end in a natural way)**.**

378

I just found a car for me. Woohoo! (= extremely satisfied)

379

I will give it best beginning today (= will do my best starting today)**.**

380

She felt compelled (= obligated) **to apologize the harm she had done.**

381

They tried hard to make her feel welcomed (= to convince her)**.**

382

She developed a passion (= a strong feeling of love) **for opera.**

383

Music, golf and writing have always been his passion (= a strong feeling of enthusiasm)**.**

384

It really pains me (= hurts me) **to ask for assistance.**

385

Don't let the stress of daily life get you down (= depress, demoralize)**.**

386

The working in the garden was a sanctuary (= felt relaxed) **from the problems of daily life.**

387

He begs (= ask in a very serious and emotional way) **to do his favor in a roughly hourlong phone call.**

388

He got many medical problems, chief among which (= main problem) **is hypertension.**

389

Those kids are in good hands (= under the safe care)**.**

390

In the clip you watched he was seen in black shirts (= seen wearing black shirts)**.**

391

The news of him served as a springboard (= something that makes begin an activity) **for a class discussion.**

392

The quick approval served as a springboard (= something that helps start process) **to expedite the project.**

393

There was a sense of surprise in the room (=everyone in the room felt surprised).

394

I will not allow you to do this, only over my dead body (=do everything you can do to prevent it).

395

He is trying to squeeze shoehorn (=compress into an insufficient space) **one hundred of us into that tiny room.**

396

He spoke in a deadpan tone (=without showing any emotions, any feelings).

397

I want you to level with me (=tell me the truth).

398

We play by the rules (=comply with the rules, follow the rules).

399

It is surprisingly painless (= no pain).

400

People want results, not revolution (= a solution, not just a change)

401

He is back in the spotlight (= public attention).

402

You make it memorable (= something to remember).

403

Eventually (= in the end) **they will be officially declared the next president and vice-president.**

404

What they did was largely ceremonial (= done as part of a ceremony).

405

He has a stake in the restaurant (= he owns part of the restaurant).

406

The base turnout helped flip (= overturn, change) **the election.**

407

They are not taking anything for granted (= accept something without questioning).

408

So far, fall short of expectation (= failed to meet, far below goal).

409

That's around the corner (= coming soon, near the place).

410

The facts are not on their side (= facts do not support them).

411

He talked about what he went through in painstaking details (= with great care and effort)**.**

412

He often moans and groans about his salary (= express unhappiness)**.**

413

It is true in a sense (= partly true or true in a general way)**.**

414

He is too bossy (= enjoy telling people what to do)**.**

415

At last (= after much delay)**, he did too little too late** (= you are blaming someone for not doing enough) **to prevent a problem and for taking action only after the problem got worse.**

416

We hope to bring home (= make people understand clearly) **the message that smoking is harmful to your health.**

417

He spotted a typo (= typing mistake) **in his essay.**

418

He put me on the spot (= a difficult position)**.**

419

The soap is scented (= having a pleasing smell)**.**

420

To bypass (= avoid) **the city's slow traffic, take the highway that circles it.**

421

The island's lifeblood (= being necessary for continuing existence) **has always been its fishing industry.**

422

As they heard the team's star player was injured, it sort of knocked the wind out of their sails (= caused to feel less confident, diminish enthusiasm).

423

The artists got short-changed (= cheated) **by people who stream music without paying.**

424

Let's get some upbeat music (= positive and cheerful).

425

I told you that from day one (= ever since the first day) **that this method would never work.**

426

When you criticize someone, sometimes it is better to take a subtle approach (= indirect, not obvious, not showing real purpose).

427

It is a bit of race against time (=must finish or do quickly) **since the deadline is tomorrow.**

428

The problem calls for a rethink (=think it over) **of what you have done. You really have to do some serious rethinking.**

429

Much to my regret (=I regret to tell you that)**, I have decided not to do that project.**

430

They had to thread their way through (=move through narrow spaces) **the crowd.**

431

It is a tough negotiation. Nobody gives in, so you have to thread the needle (=find a striking balance)**.**

432

His article is a good analysis of the political pulse (=feelings, opinions) of young voters.

433

The price you paid for the car seems to be fair enough (=reasonable, acceptable).

434

I will cut a check (=write a check) for the balance due tomorrow.

435

It seems to me that helping the needy now outweighs (=exceed in importance) all others, but still we are debating whether that is a good idea.

436

The delivery of that package on time is very important to me. Please don't bungle (=make mistakes, botch) it.

437

The early poll shows that the races are anyone's to win (= anyone can win)**.**

438

You can spot egregious (= glaring, easily noticeable) **errors in the article he authored.**

439

A quiet weather pattern (= no storm, no strong wind or rain) **is on the horizon. Temperatures will be seasonable, and this trend will extend into the next month.**

440

During the speech the candidate spewed out (= spoke in a forceful way) **lies, conspiracy theories and nonsensically false claims.**

441

It is gratifying to have a friend in the know (= having inside information) **about important people.**

442

It is extremely difficult race to win as a Democratic candidate. His win will be nothing short of a miracle (= equivalent to).

443

He tangles (= fight, argue) with a reporter.

444

My barber took his time (= slowly and carefully without hurrying) cutting my hair and did really a good job.

445

Feel alive (= having life), perhaps one would say it when he or she feels happy about what is being done every day (= satisfactory life).

446

It is a very difficult situation. You have to find a way to thread a needle (= skillfully navigate through).

447

He sang perfectly on pitch, but was a little off pitch (= too high or too low) **on the last note.**

448

This act is usually a formality (= required, but has little importance)**.**

449

The lion's share (= the larger part) **of that win went to her.**

450

He got the lion's share of the blame (= most of the blame) **for failure.**

451

His political future is hanging by a thread (= very uncertain, in a risky or unstable situation) **due to the recent revelation of his gambling problem.**

452

See how many people are on board (= joining in, participating) with us on that proposal.

453

Sorry. I was going to call you right back, but got sidetracked (= distracted, prevented) because of a fire alarm.

454

Is there anything in the pipeline (= in process)?

455

It is important to know about do's and don'ts (= should and should not) when you host a reception.

456

He has a fertile mind (= producing many ideas). What worries me is his fertile mind of finding fraud where none exists (= delusional).

457

It is nice to have this win. This will mark a triumphant coda (=end) **for his 2020 campaign.**

458

The two wins in that state runoffs will shift control of U.S. Senate, handing (=giving) **the control to the other party.**

459

I saw with my own eyes (=saw it myself) **how much he has changed.**

460

You were there when the accident happened. Please give us a firsthand (=directly coming from actually seeing something) **account of what caused it.**

461

It is shaping up (=develop in a particular way) **to be a very busy day for me. I am going to be surrounded by many people.**

462

We saw hours of chaos and violence occurring in the city yesterday. It will go down (= recorded, going to be) as one of the darkest day in the city's political history.

463

If he is found guilty of that kind of crime, it will disqualify him from ever (= forever) holding office again.

464

I looked on in shock (= unpleasantly surprised) at the violence that took place yesterday in the city.

465

His refusal to accept reality (= facts) led me to concern. We worry over what he may do.

466

I decided to do it after a lot of soul-searching. (= deep consideration).

467

He has been spreading falsehoods online over the years, prompting criticism that they should have done more, and sooner, to stop him from stoking (=causing) **real world tensions.**

468

Facing calls for his removal from office, he reverses his positions on that issue. That is a striking shift (=unusual turn)**.**

469

He is trying to get the most out of (=the greatest output possible) **his employees.**

470

He is doing a good job running (=managing) **a small family-owned business.**

471

He is reluctant to do what has usually been done by his predecessors, breaking from tradition (= not following) **at a time everyone looks for unity.**

472

He has broken all previous records (= the things that have done in the past)**, even breaking a record set just one day before.**

473

He changes policy by stealth (= a secret, quiet way)**, skipping** (= avoiding) **necessary consultation.**

474

They lost the game. The players dejectedly (= sadly, depressingly) **walked off the field** (= left the field)**.**

475

The defendant (= the person accused of the wrongdoing) **entered the courtroom. The term defendant is a technical term** (= lingo) **that is used by someone who works in a specific field can understand.**

476

Please put such a complex and technical statement in layman's terms (= simple ordinary language that everyone can understand).

477

The article has a lot of computer lingo (= a particular word that is used in a specific field) **that is difficult to comprehend.**

478

The police arrested the man seen carrying a bomb (= shown) **during the height** (= peak) **of the violence.**

479

I think it is better to take frequent breaks to avoid burn out (=mental, physical exhaustion).

480

It is abundantly (=amply) obvious that we will have a lot of problem to find a solution for this one.

481

Hey, stop pushing me (=forcing me) into this lousy agreement. I am not happy with the deal.

482

He crashed his car, but somehow, he managed to limp it along (=move slowly) to the garage.

483

The new vaccine (=substance for injection, medicine) is a beacon of hope (=a hopeful sign) to thousands of patients.

484
He got the information by combing (= search thoroughly) **through his diary.**

485
We should try to harness (= make use of) **the skill and creativity of our employees to enhance our current technologies.**

486
When they realized that they are barricaded (= blocked in) **in a small room they sounded** (= shouted) **urgent pleas for help.**

487
He has been pilloried (= publicly criticized) **by both parties for pushing the futile effort.**

488
His dismissal was a long time coming (= overdue)**.**

489

The company alleges that its efforts to improve efficiency is being hamstrung (=render ineffective) **by government interferences.**

490

You are up to speed (=updated with the latest information) **now. Let's start doing some work.**

491

He acts like he is a real macho (=masculine) **man.**

492

If you do just do your stuff (=the things that you able to do well) **you would be all right.**

493

New interesting ideas are always bubbling up (=becoming known) **all over the country.**

494

He seems to be mindless (=not aware of) **of the fact that he will encounter** (=face) **a very difficult situation.**

495

There was a palpable (=noticeable) **excitement in the air as we welcome a new year.**

496

Based on the fact you cited, I guess I am partially (=partly, somewhat but not completely) **responsible for that mishap** (=an unlucky mistake)**.**

497

I like all the food here on the table, but I am partial to (=prefer) **the Kimchee.**

498

He did a lot of controversial things and becomes a magnet (=something that attracts) **for criticism.**

499

You gave the right answer. You hit it (=gave wanted answer, exactly right)**, bingo. Congratulations!**

500

The guy was given an ultimatum (=uncompromising demand)-**work harder or don't come back.**